Quilling Art

Learn how to Quill for Beginners with Simple Patterns

Copyright © 2020

All rights reserved.

DEDICATION

The author and publisher have provided this e-book to you for your personal use only. You may not make this e-book publicly available in any way. Copyright infringement is against the law. If you believe the copy of this e-book you are reading infringes on the author's copyright, please notify the publisher at: https://us.macmillan.com/piracy

Contents

Start with these 29 Rolled-Paper Shapes 1

    1. Insert Paper into the Tool 3

    2. Start Rollin' 4

    3. Glue It 5

Candy Jar Project 36

Valentine Card 42

Quilling Flowers 49

Paper Quilling Fall 59

Start with these 29 Rolled-Paper Shapes

We're way into the new craze called quilling. "Craze" is an unlikely word to describe a craft that dates back to the Renaissance, but whatever — it's trending.

In case you don't know, quilling has nothing to do with hedgehogs or feather pens. It's a paper craft that involves rolling narrow strips of paper into unique 3D shapes. These little paper forms can then be used to decorate greeting cards, pictures, gift bags and boxes, or glued together to make mosaics, sculptures and other works of art.

And here's why we heart it so much: Quilling is creative, easy, fun, inexpensive and, once you get on a roll (ha), incredibly relaxing.

It's also pretty addicting — which is why we're giving you the ways on how to make dozens of different shapes. Pretty soon you'll want to be quilling and chilling all the time.

What You Need

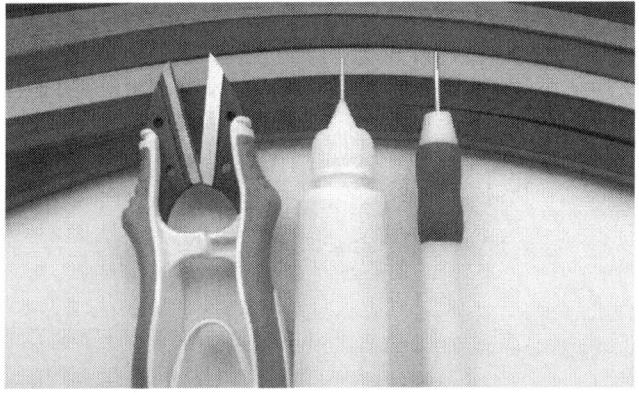

- A slotted quilling tool
- Quilling glue in a needle-tip bottle

- Scissors

- Tweezers

- Package of quilling paper strips — for beginners, I recommend ¼-inch wide (it's easy to grip and manipulate); once you've mastered the basic shapes, you may prefer narrower strips. Cut the strips 8½-inches long for this tutorial.

Open and Closed Coils

Simple circles are the basis for most other shapes you'll create.

1. Insert Paper into the Tool

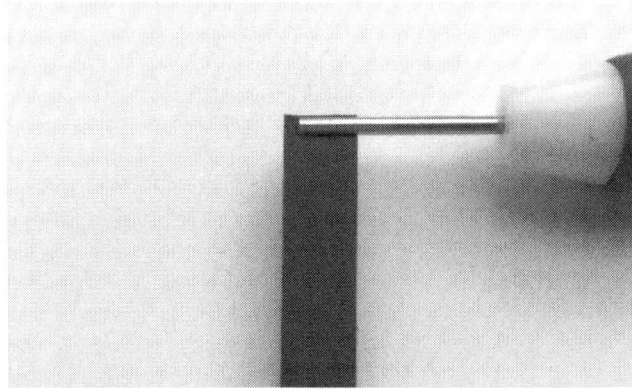

Insert a piece of quilling paper into the slot of your quilling tool; try to line up the edge of the paper with the edge of the slot as perfectly as you can. A slotted tool will naturally leave a small crimp in the center of your coil. If you'd like the crimp to be more visible, allow the paper to hang slightly over the edge.

2. Start Rollin'

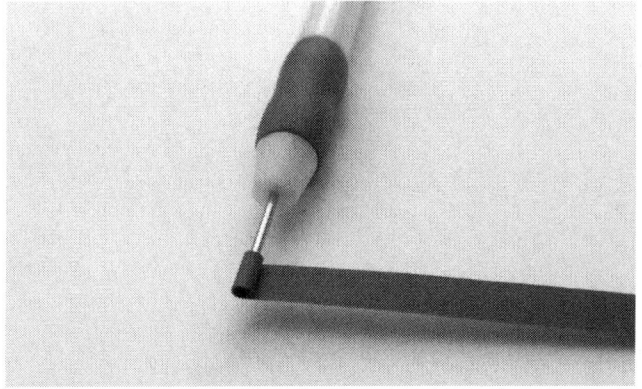

Roll the tool with your dominant hand either towards your body or away from it (whichever feels most comfortable), while holding the strip taut with your other hand.

3. Glue It

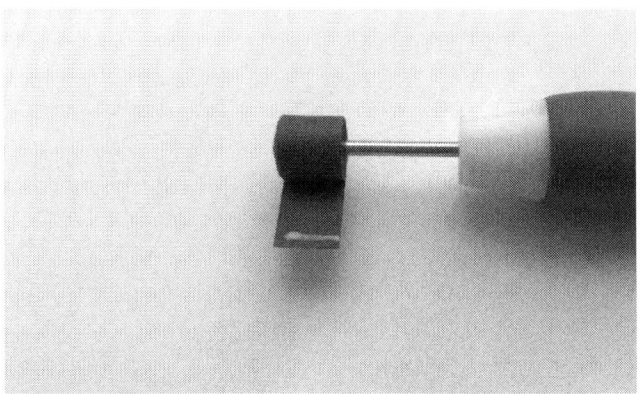

For a closed coil: When you're almost done coiling, place a dab of glue near the end of the strip and roll to complete. You don't want it to expand after you remove it from the tool.

Quilling Art

For an open coil: Finish the coil, then remove it from the tool and allow it to expand. Once it has fully expanded, add a dab of glue and press the strip down carefully to secure.

Teardrop

Make an open coil, then place it between the thumb and forefinger of your non-dominant hand. Arrange the inside coils evenly or however you'd like.

Quilling Art

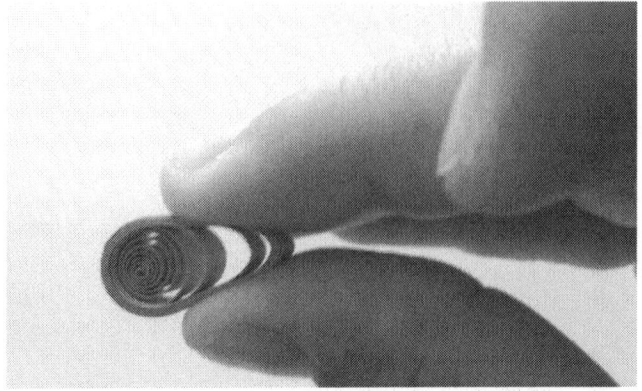

With your dominant hand, pinch the paper where you want the point to be to create a teardrop shape.

Teardrop Variations

Basic shapes can be manipulated to create even more shapes. The teardrop is an excellent example of this.

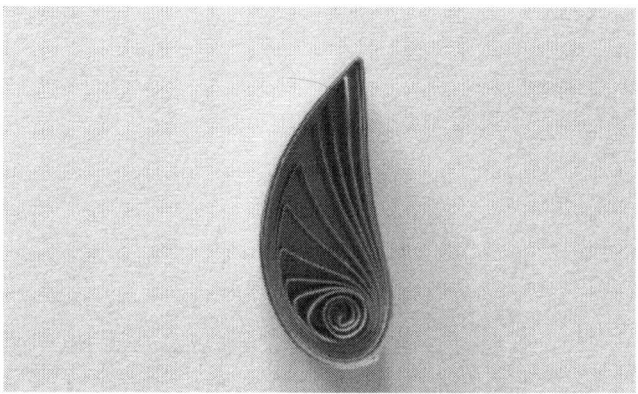

By slightly curving the teardrop around your thumb as you shape it, you can create a subtle shift in form without compromising the center coils. To exaggerate this effect, you can wrap the teardrop around your quilling tool or another cylindrical object.

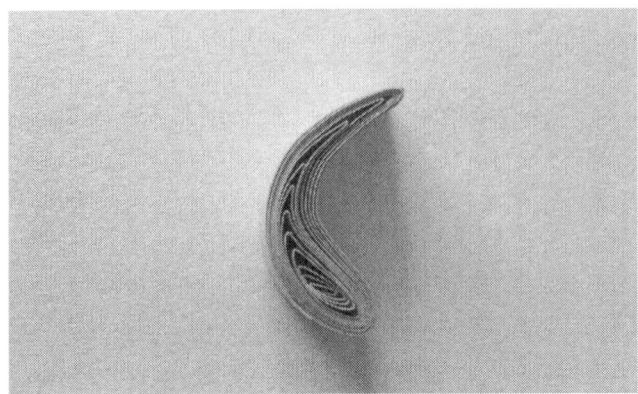

For a more obvious curved shape throughout, press the shape around your quilling tool. From here, you can easily create a paisley shape.

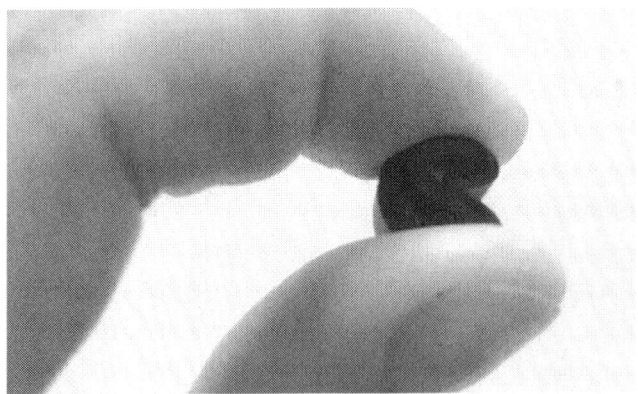

You can curl the shape from the point to the base by rolling it between your fingers.

So many shapes!

Marquis

First make a teardrop shape, then pinch the opposite end as well.

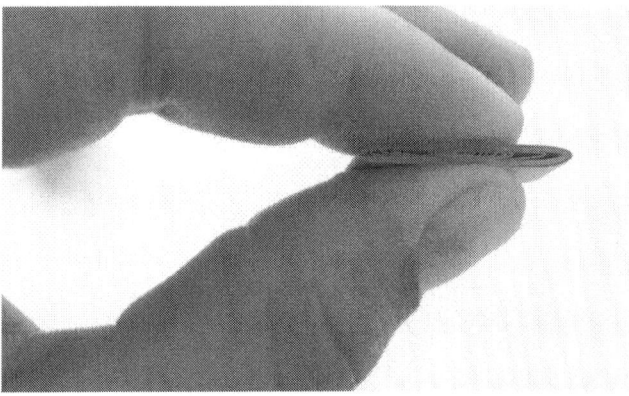

The final shape will be determined by how much you pinch or press the the coil together and where you place its center.

Quilling Art

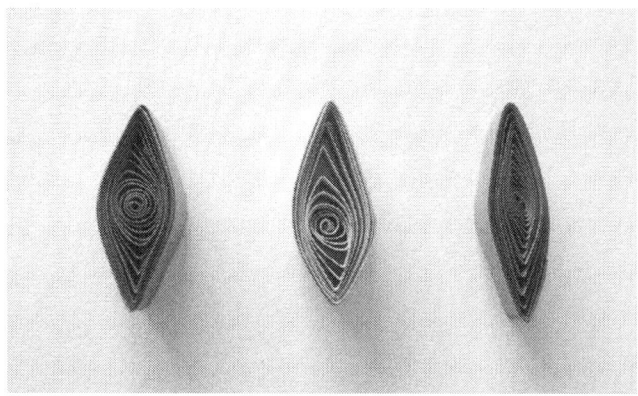

Play around with different placements and pressure to create lots of marquis versions.

Tulip

First make a marquis shape, then turn the shape on its side and pinch a center peak with your fingers.

Slug

Start with a marquis, then wrap one end around the tip of your finger or a quilling tool.

Quilling Art

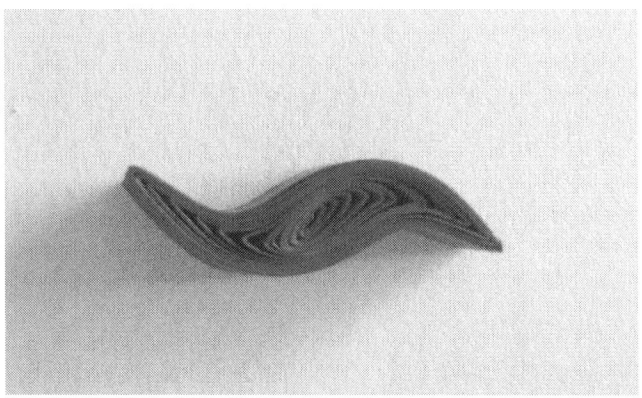

Do the same to the other end but in the opposite direction. Looks pretty for a slug, doesn't it!

Square or Diamond

Quilling Art

Create a marquis shape, then rotate it 90 degrees and pinch both sides again. This will create a diamond shape.

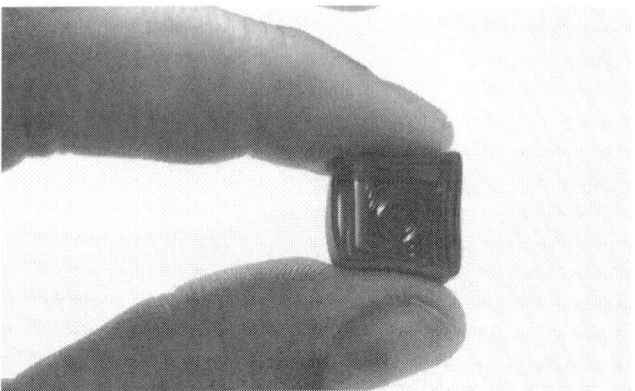

If you want to continue on to making a square, gently open up the shape between your fingers.

Square Variations

By playing around with how much of each corner you choose to pinch when creating your square, you can get very different results.

Above left: By applying pressure to the outside corners, you can create a square with a rounded center.

Above center: This was made by completely pressing the open coil together on one side, then opening it up and pinching just the corners on the opposite side.

Above right: This got its unique center by completely pressing down the coil on both turns.

Yet another variation on the square: You can make these by applying pressure to the outside structure with your fingers or the stem of your quilling tool.

Rectangle

Quilling Art

If you can make a square, you can make a rectangle. The difference is in how much you rotate the marquis shape before pinching additional angles.

Rotate it only slightly (rather than 90 degrees) before pinching and then open the shape to reveal the perfect rectangle.

Rectangle Variations

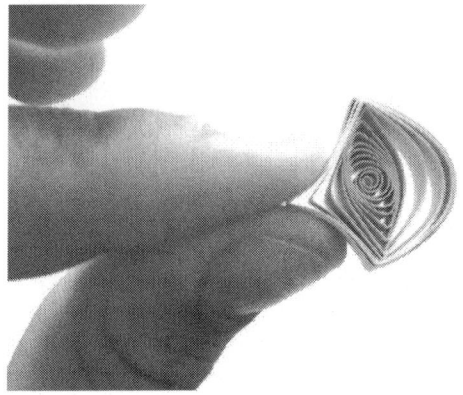

Alternately, you can create a quadrilateral shape by making your four corners at uneven intervals.

Quilling Art

This shape is especially useful when you're making quilled paper mosaics and you need to fill in an odd space.

Semi-Circle

Quilling Art

Start with an open coil, then pinch two corners while leaving the paper above them round. You can also do this by pressing an open coil onto a hard surface like a table and sliding your fingers down the sides carefully. Try both methods to see which suits you best.

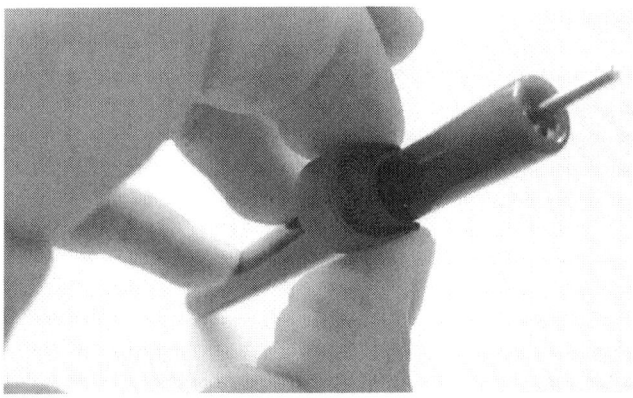

Quilling Art

Curving the straight edge of the shape will allow you to turn a semi-circle into more of a crescent moon shape.

Triangle

Make a teardrop shape, then pinch two additional angles using either your fingers or the tabletop method.

Once again, try both to see what works best for you.

Triangle Variation

To create a shape that resembles a shark fin, press in two sides of your triangle and leave the third side flat.

Arrow

Quilling Art

Make a teardrop, then pull the center down towards the base and hold it in place with your fingers.

Using the long side of the slotted needle, press down deeply into the base.

Quilling Art

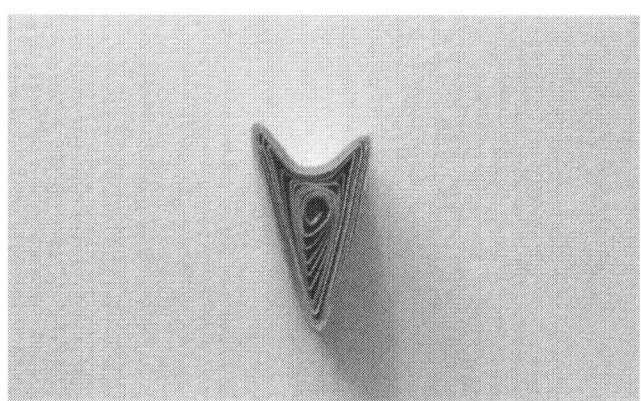

Release the tool and smooth the curve out with your fingers to shape.

Arrowhead

Beginning with a teardrop shape, hold the pointed end in your non-dominant hand and pinch the base end into a tight point.

Without letting go, slide your fingers down to meet the fingers of your opposite hand to create the side angles.

Heart

Quilling Art

Once again, begin with a teardrop. Press in the base of the shape by using the point of your quilling tool to make a small indentation.

Release the tool and carefully press in each side of the heart to complete the center crease.

Pentagon and Star

To make a pentagon, first create an elongated semi-circle as

shown above.

Pinch the center of the flat side using the same method you used when making the tulip shape; this is the peak of your pentagon.

Keeping the peak in the center, square off the bottom with two equal pinches on either side.

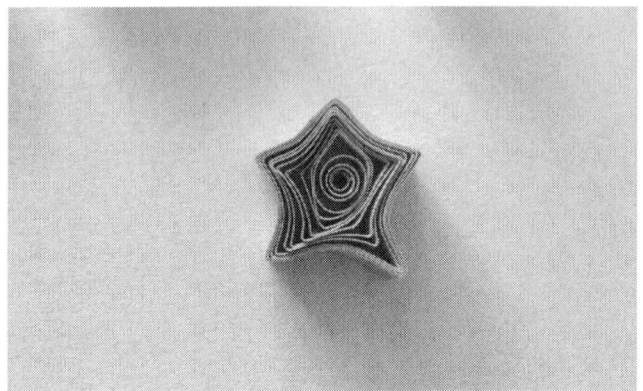

To turn the pentagon into a star, press in on each flat surface with your fingers or a quilling tool and then further refine each angle into peaks.

Holly Leaf

Quilling Art

This shape is far and away the most difficult to create. For sanity's sake, you'll want to become comfortable making all of the other shapes before attempting this one!

Begin by making a marquis. Insert a set of tweezers into the shape; try to grip only about a third of the inside coil.

Quilling Art

Keeping the grip with your tweezers, turn the marquis as needed and pinch a small point on either side of each peak.

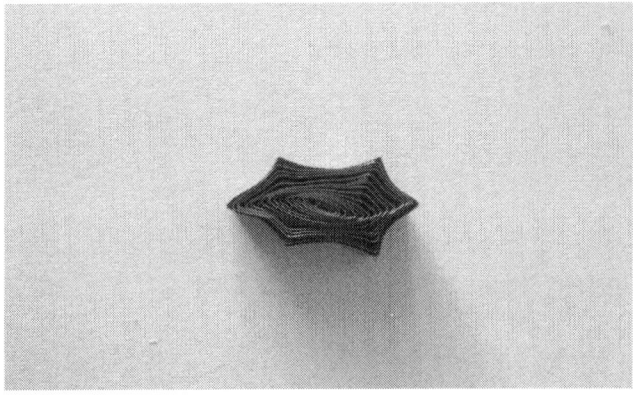

You could also make the holly leaf by first making a square, adding a point to each end and then shaping all the angles into peaks. I find the tweezer method easier, but try both ways to see which gives you better results.

Now that you've seen a bunch of shapes, imagine how you'd use them together to create designs. Welcome to the world of quilling!

Quilling Art

Candy Jar Project

Quilling Art

Materials:

Glass jar

Grosgrain ribbon – red, 3/8"

Quilling paper, red, 1/8"

Cardstock, white

Adhesive foam dots

Directions

Quilling Art

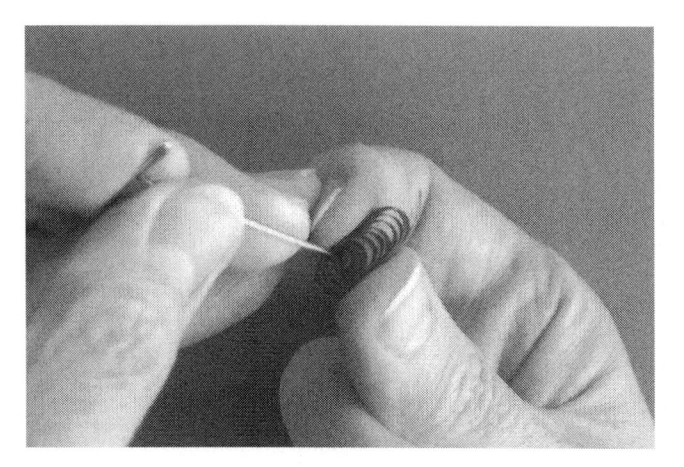

Step 1: Make 4 teardrop. Roll a 12" loose coil. Press the coil slightly between your fingers, and, if necessary, use a pin to arrange the inner coils so they are evenly spaced.

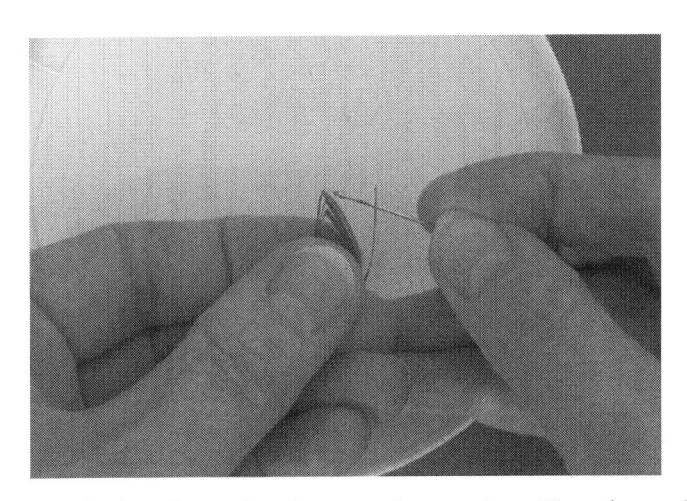

Pinch sharply at the tip to make a point. Glue the end and trim the excess paper.

Quilling Art

Step 2: Make 2 hearts. Place 2 teardrops side by side on the work board to create a heart shape, positioning them in opposite directions so the inner coils appear to meet. Apply glue at the join spot.

Quilling Art

Hold the teardrops in place with pins while the glue dries.

Step 3: Fill a jar with your favorite treat and tie a ribbon around it.

Step 4: Cut 2 white, 1" cardstock squares and glue a heart on each.

Tip: When gluing a quilled object on a background, spread a shallow puddle of glue on a plastic container lid or a sheet of waxed paper. Hold the quilling with tweezers and dip its underside gently in glue. Place directly on the background.

Step 5: Attach 1 square to each ribbon tail with a glue dot.

Valentine Card

Materials:

Cardstock, red

Watercolor digital paper

Printer quilling paper, red, 1/8"

Twill tape, white, 1/2"

Paper clip, red

Jewelry pliers, 2 flat-nose

Jump rings, 2 silver

Clear message sticker

Glue stick

Paper cutter

Printer

Directions:

Step 1: Score and fold a 7½"x5½" piece of red cardstock to make a 3¾"x5½" card.

Step 2: Print out the digital watercolor background and cut it to measure 3¼"x5". Use a glue stick to adhere the rectangle to the center of the card.

Step 3: Outline the patterned paper with quilling strips. Overlap the strips squarely at the corners or miter at a slant as shown, following my tutorial.

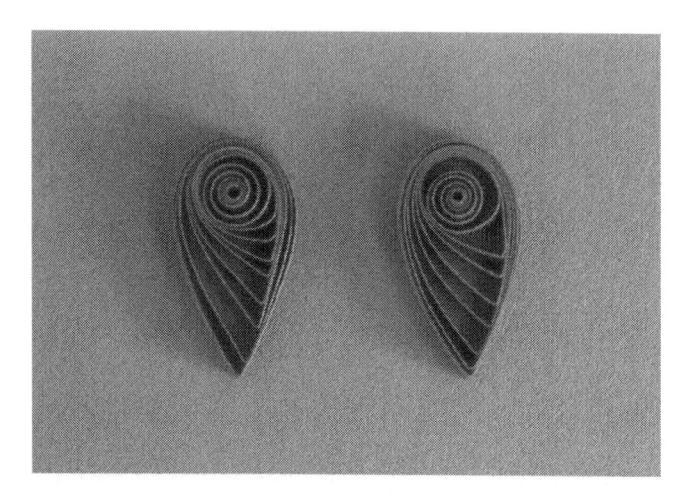

Step 4: Make a heart (2 teardrops). Each teardrop requires a full-length strip, 24". Position the teardrops so that the inner coils face in the same direction. (This is opposite of the way the candy jar teardrops were positioned.) Facing the coils in the same direction will give a nice look when shaping the curve. Glue the teardrops side by side, pinning them in place on the work board until dry.

Quilling Art

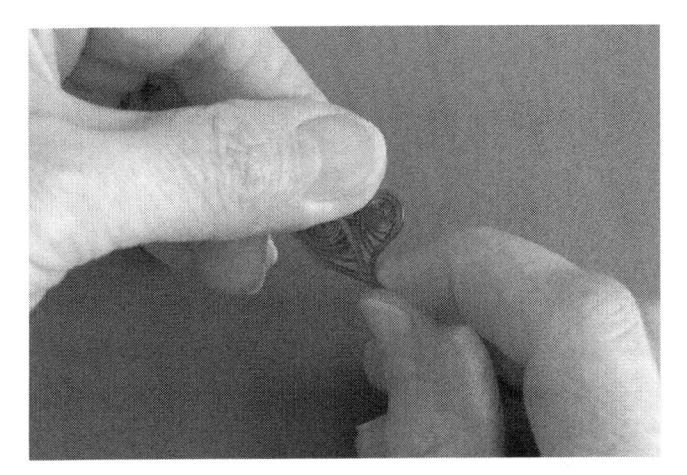

Step 5: Grasp the tip of the heart and curve it gently.

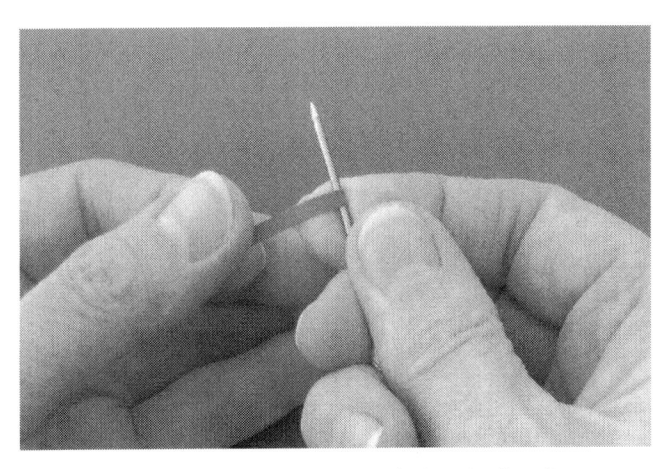

Step 6: Roll a 2½" strip around the shaft of a paper piercing tool or round toothpick to make a bead. Glue the torn end.

Quilling Art

Tip: A torn end blends better than a blunt cut.

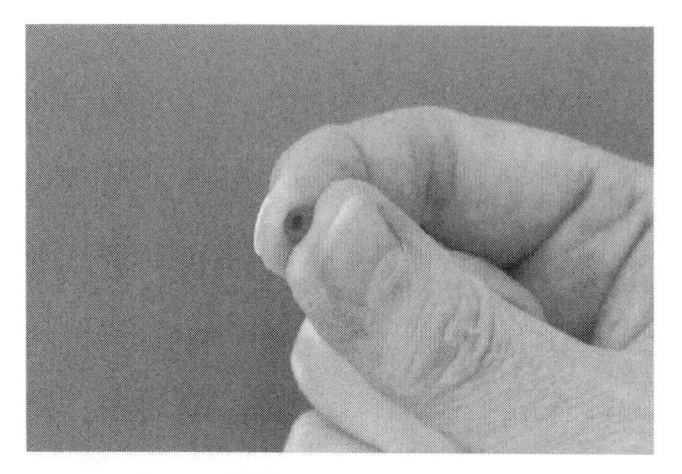

Step 7: Pinch the bead to form an oval ring coil.

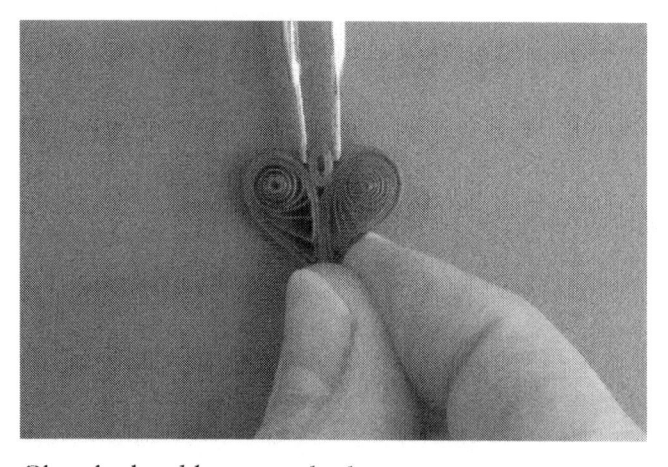

Glue the bead between the heart curves.

Step 8: Use pliers to open 2 jump rings and attach them to the ring coil.

Step 9: Slip the jump ring onto the paper clip.

Step 10: Cut a ¾"-wide strip of cardstock to fit the width of the card between the bordered edges, and glue it in place, covering the lettering on the printed digital paper.

Step 11: Cut twill tape to the same length as the cardstock strip. Slide the paper clip/heart onto the twill tape. Center and glue the twill tape onto the cardstock strip.

Step 12: Press on a clear sticker message. I used "Celebrate"; the inside message could read "our love" or "with the one you love." And of course, Happy Valentine's Day!

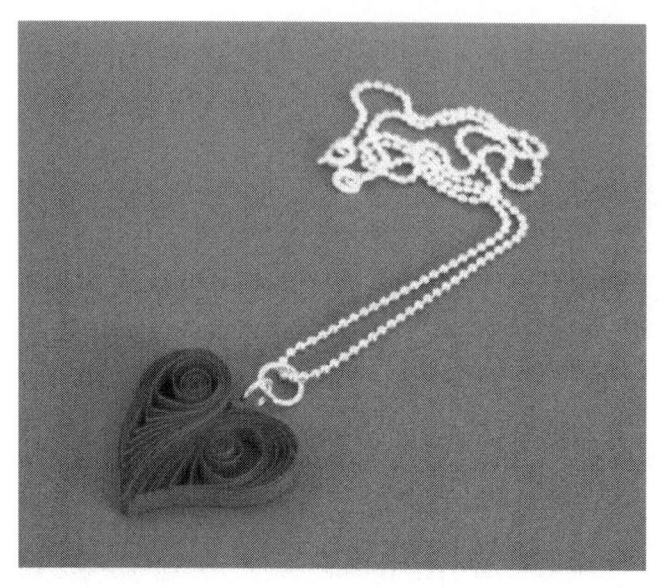

As a variation, add a chain and wear the quilled heart as a necklace pendant. If desired, spray the heart with a satin finish acrylic varnish to give it water resistance and extra durability.

Quilling Art

Quilling Flowers

Total Time: 60 mins

Yield: 3 quilled flowers

Skill Level: Intermediate

What You'll Need

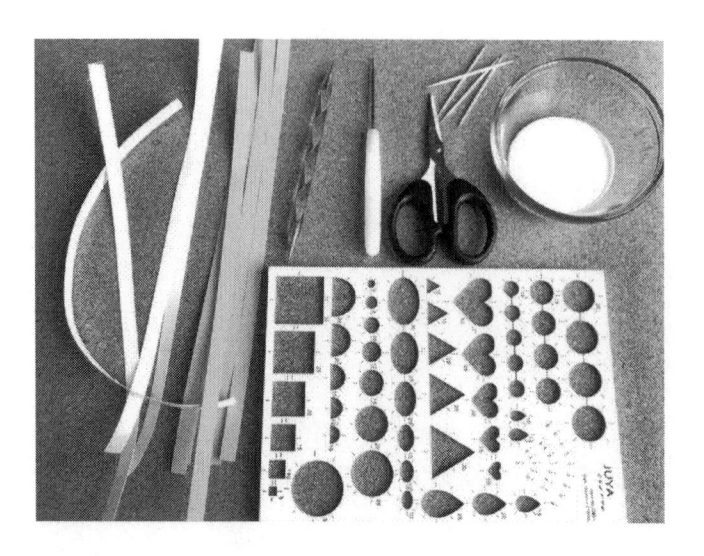

Equipment / Tools

- Quilling board
- Slotted quilling tool
- Needle quilling tool
- Toothpicks
- Scissors
- Paper trimmer/cutter (if cutting paper strips by hand)
- Craft glue

- Straight pins (optional)
- Hot glue (optional)
- Tweezers (optional)
- Ruler (optional)

Materials

- Paper for strips or pre-cut paper quilling strips approximately
- Small flower pot (optional)
- Floral foam (optional)
- Thin wood dowels or wood skewers (optional)
- Artificial Spanish moss (optional)

Instructions

1. Construct the Daisy Petals

You will need to cut six white paper strips to make the daisy petals.

Cut strips to measure 3/8 inches wide by 12 inches long. If you are using pre-cut quilling paper strips, you may need to cut them down.

To make a paper petal, you first have to take a piece of paper and insert it into the slot of the slotted quilling tool.

Hold the tool in your hand between your thumb and index finger and slowly turn the tool so the paper winds evenly around the tip.

Pull the coil from the tool and place it into a circle on the quilling board, and allow the coil to unwind until it is the size of the circle.

Remove the paper coil and glue the end of the strip and let it dry. You may then squeeze the paper coil into different shapes.

Using a Template Board

Our board is sized in millimeters, and we used the 25-millimeter circle template, which is a little under 1 inch. If your template board has circles sized in inches, use the 1-inch circle template for your petals.

Quilling Art

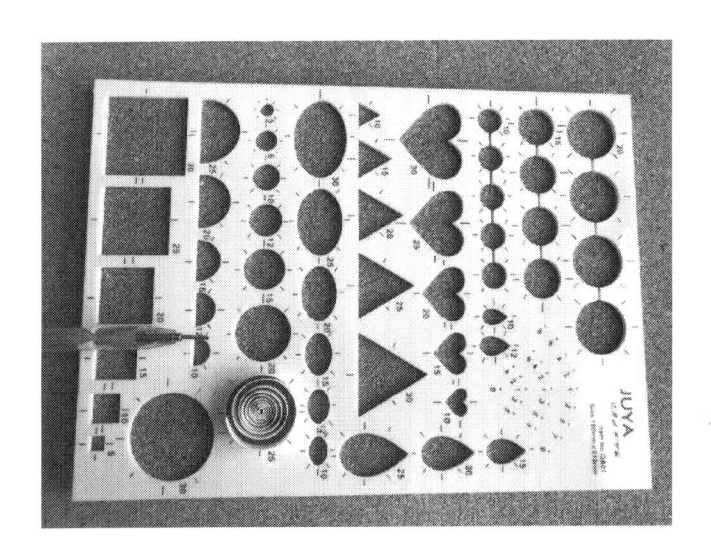

2. Squeeze the Paper Coil into a Teardrop Shape

To form a paper coil into a teardrop shape, you must first pull the inside of the coil gently downwards and hold while pinching one side of the circle to form a point. Your paper circle will now be in a teardrop shape.

Make six paper teardrop shapes to form the petals of your quilled daisy.

3. Make the Center of the Daisy

To make the center of the daisy, you will need two colored paper strips (each about 3/8 inch wide and 12 inches long) and the slotted tool.

Thread one end of the paper strip into the slot and turn the tool making sure to maintain tension.

After you form the center coil place some glue on the end of the paper strip and let it dry. Do not remove the coil from the tool.

Place a bit of glue onto the rolled coil and place another paper strip aligned with the end of the first paper strip.

Roll the second paper strip onto the coil, maintaining tension.

Add some glue to the end of the second paper strip.

Let the glue dry.

Remove the tight coil from the slotted tool.

4. Glue Together Your Quilled Shapes

Arrange the six teardrop petals around the paper coil to form the flower shape.

Glue the teardrops to the paper coil and to the sides of each teardrop shape.

Let the glue completely dry.

After the flower dries you will be able to pick it up and it should hold its shape.

Gluing Quills in Place

There are many tips on how to handle delicate quilled parts. Here are two tips that help when gluing them together.

1. Tweezers makes it easier to arrange the small quills into place and while gluing them together.

2. Using straight pins helps to keep the quilled rolls in place until the glue dries.

5. Plant Your Flowers

Quilled flowers can be used in card projects, scrapbooking, wall hangings, and as welcoming signs of springtime. Here's how we displayed our flowers in a flowerpot:

Hot glue some thin wooden dowels or skewers onto the back of the flowers.

Place dry floral foam into a small flower pot.

Stick the flowers on wood "stems" into the floral foam.

Quilling Art

Cover the top of the pot opening with artificial Spanish moss — what a delightful way to welcome spring or summer!

Paper Quilling Fall

List of Supplies

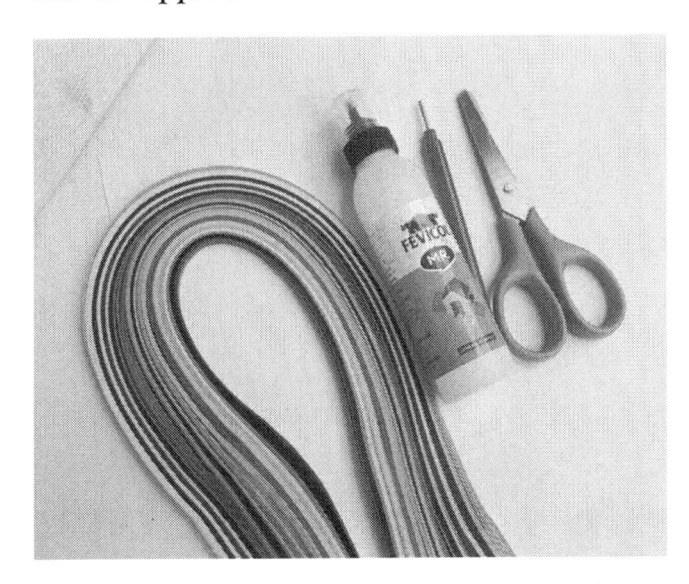

1. Quilling paper strips – 5mm – Red, Yellow, Orange, Brown

2. White cardstock 6 x 12 inches

3. Craft glue

4. Slotted quilling tool

5. Scissors

Quilling Art

Instructions:

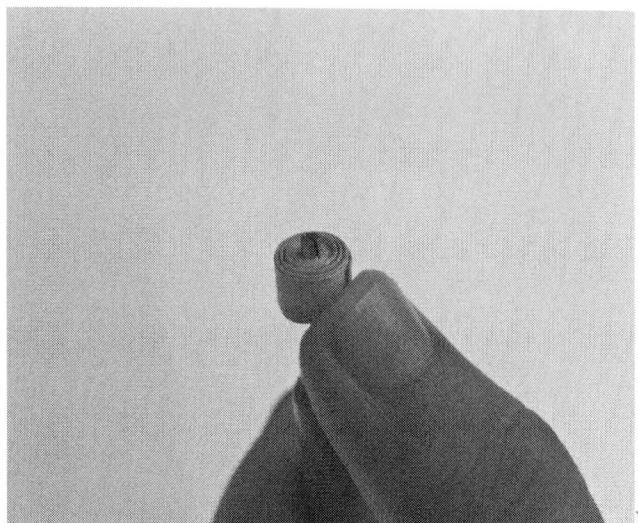

I'm so done

Select 3-4 fall colored quilling strips. Take a 10-inch long quilling strip and coil the entire strip with the help of the slotted quilling tool.

Take out the coiled strip out of the slotted tool and allow the coil to loosen up a little. Glue the open end to secure the loose coil shape.

Quilling Art

Press any one side of the loose coil prepared in the previous step to create a teardrop shape. We have created a teardrop shape.

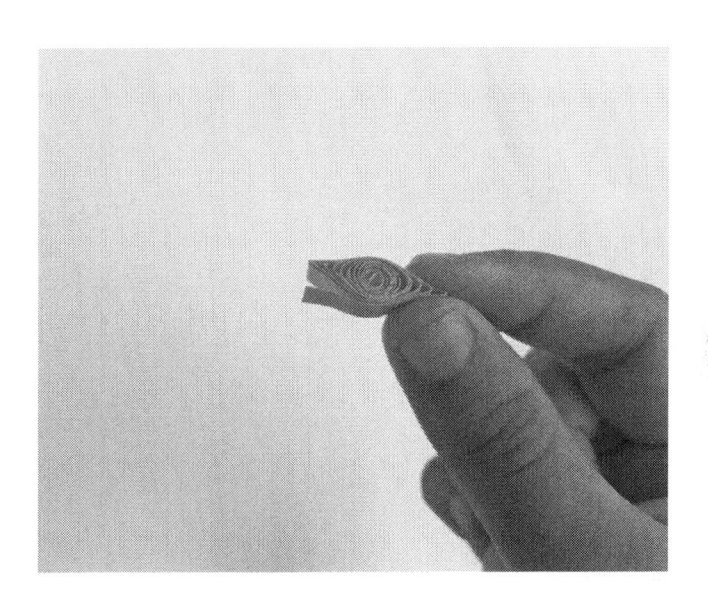

Now press the opposite side of the coils' previously pressed side to create a basic eye shape. Glue the open end of the strip to secure the shape.

Quilling Art

Similarly, create more basic eye shapes using fall colored quilling strips. These will be the leaves.

Take brown colored quilling strips and cut them into any customized size you want, mine were 5 inches long. Use the slotted tool to coil about 1 or 1.5 inches of the strip from any one end.

Quilling Art

Similarly, prepare 6 to 8 more strips as prepared in the previous step.

Fold a piece of white cardstock paper in half to form a card.. Glue the strips prepared in step 7 on the paper; basically creating the trunk of the tree.

Now take the basic eye shapes (leaves) and start to stick them above the trunk pattern.

Quilling Art

While sticking the leaf shapes try to keep a nice pattern combination. I glued 3 to 4 basic eye shapes in groups.

Quilling Art

All done? You can stop once you are satisfied with the tree pattern. Allow the glue to dry.

Quilling Art

And done!

71